is to be returned on or before th

First published in Great Britain in 2011
and the USA in 2012 by
Frances Lincoln Children's Books,
74-77 White Lion Street
London. N1 9PF
www.franceslincoln.com

Photographs by
Jan Panke: cover, pages 4-13, 36-40, 43
Sophie Pelham: cover, pages 4-7, 14-19, 26-28, 41, 42
Nicholas Posner: cover, pages 2-7, 20-25, 30-35, 43
p32 top photograph: thefinalmiracle © Fotolia
p29 photographs © Amaravati Buddhist Monastery

A catalogue record for this book is available
from the British Library.

ISBN 978-1-84507-986-4

Set in Futura BT

Printed in Shenzhen, Guangdong, China
by C&C Offset in July 2015
3 5 7 9 8 6 4 2

For Anthony, Isaac and Emily – S.R.
For Dan, Lottie and Poppy – S.P.

Acknowledgements

We would like to thank the following
people for their invaluable help in
creating this book:

Francesca Rigg, Janie Bickersteth and
family, Jacob and Debra Virchis and family,
Aneesa and Julie Ali and family,
Francis and Mashya Fumagali, Akhil and
Rachna Gupta and family, Tavleen Kaur,
Kanwaljit Kaur Singh and family,
Reverend Fred Woods, Rabbi Jonathan
Wittenberg, Shama Husain,
Bhikkhu Ahimsako and all at Amaravati
Buddhist Monastery, Rasamandala Das,
South London Sikh Gurdwara, Newcastle
Hindu Temple, Dr Anthony Bash, Hatfield
College, University of Durham, Ranbir
Kaur, Seaburn Centre, Sunderland, Ruth
Simmons, Kosher Deli Temple Fortune,
Raficq Abdulla, Farmida Bi, Hannah and
Matthew Hawes, Nicola and
Lawrence Clarke, Jo and Shaun Cobley,
Sarah Manson, Alexei Charkham,
and finally, Cathy Herbert,
whose idea this was in the first place.

FOOD
AND FAITH

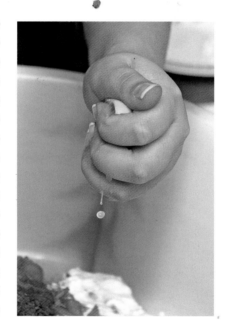

SUSAN REUBEN AND SOPHIE PELHAM

PHOTOGRAPHY BY
JAN PANKE, SOPHIE PELHAM AND NICHOLAS POSNER

My name is FRANCESCA. I am CHRISTIAN.

I am 10 years old. I play the trombone and piano, and I love dancing and sport. My favourite time of year is Christmas – I like decorating the Christmas tree, making mince pies and eating turkey sandwiches on Boxing Day!

My name is JACOB. I am JEWISH.

I am 11 years old. I go to a Jewish school, and in my spare time I like skateboarding, dance and football. I enjoy baking *challah* (the bread we eat on Friday night) because it's fun to make it into lots of different shapes.

My name is ANEESA. I am MUSLIM.

I am 11 years old and I enjoy cooking, swimming, reading and sketching my own henna designs. My favourite festival is Eid, as I love getting dressed up and going out to eat at the homes of my family and friends.

CHILDREN AND THEIR FAITHS

My name is FRANCIS. I am BUDDHIST.

I am 11 years old. My hobbies are photography and playing the guitar. I like being at the Buddhist monastery because I feel free there. I have a lot of fun helping with the cooking and I enjoy offering food to the monks and nuns.

PAGES 26-29

My name is AKHIL. I am HINDU.

I am 11 years old. In my spare time I enjoy playing chess, table tennis, snooker and cricket. My favourite festival is Diwali, because my mum and grandma make such delicious food for it.

PAGES 30-35

My name is TAVLEEN. I am SIKH.

I am 10 years old. I like karate and playing the piano and clarinet. I enjoy helping to prepare meals in the gurdwara (temple) kitchen. I love the smell of the fresh spices and herbs which we add to the food as we cook it.

PAGES 36-41

We Christians eat lots of special foods at different festivals, such as turkey at Christmas, pancakes on Shrove Tuesday and chocolate eggs at Easter.

MY FAVOURITE TIME of year is Christmas, when we remember the birth of Jesus Christ, our spiritual leader. Just before Christmas, we have a Christingle service at my church. I have made my Christingle by taking an orange and sticking a candle and dried fruits into it. All the parts have different meanings.

LIGHTED CANDLE
Jesus, the Light of the World

COCKTAIL STICKS WITH SULTANAS
The four seasons and the fruits of the Earth

ORANGE
The World

RED RIBBON
The blood of Christ

WHEN WE GET HOME after the service, we make a Christmas wreath using leaves, branches and berries. It symbolises Advent – the coming of Christ.

CHRISTMAS

Class: 200 REU
Accession No: 141162
Type: 3 Weeks

IT'S CHRISTMAS EVE, the day before Christmas. I'm busy baking mince pies, which are little pastry cases filled with dried fruits. Mince pies used to be oval-shaped to represent the baby Jesus's crib, but these days they're usually round.

Before bed, my brother and I hang up a stocking in front of the fireplace. People say that Father Christmas (Saint Nicholas) will come down the chimney during the night and fill it with presents. Then I try to sleep – which is difficult, because I'm so excited that it's nearly Christmas Day!

ON CHRISTMAS MORNING my brother and I get up very early to open our presents. After that, we go to church where we sing carols, which are Christmas hymns. It's a really happy service, because we're celebrating Jesus' birth.

CHRISTIAN

CHRISTMAS DAY

WHEN WE GET HOME, it's time for everyone to sit down to Christmas dinner. Dad got up nearly as early as we did so that he could cook the turkey. Before we begin, we say Grace, which is a prayer thanking God for the meal.
This is what we have for Christmas dinner:

STUFFING
Flour, onion, butter and sage

ROAST POTATOES

TURKEY WITH GRAVY

CRANBERRY SAUCE

CARROTS

BACON

CHIPOLATA SAUSAGES

SPROUTS

SHROVE TUESDAY

THE 40 DAYS before the festival of Easter are called Lent. During this time we remember the days Jesus spent fasting in the desert, preparing to be a spiritual leader. A long time ago, Christians used to fast during Lent – they didn't eat meat or other rich foods. So the day before Lent – Shrove Tuesday – they made pancakes to use up all the fat. Nowadays we don't fast any more, though I always try to give up chocolate during Lent.

WE STILL HAVE pancakes on Shrove Tuesday. I make them by mixing up a batter with eggs, flour and milk. Then, when I've cooked the pancake on one side, I toss it in the air to turn it over. It takes a lot of practice to make sure it lands back in the pan! I like to eat my pancakes with sugar and lemon, but you can put all sorts of things on them – sweet or savoury.

GOOD FRIDAY

DURING HOLY WEEK AND EASTER, we remember when Jesus died and rose again from the dead.

THE DAY BEFORE Jesus' death, He ate a Passover meal with his followers. He told them to remember Him in future by eating bread and drinking wine, to represent His body and His blood. So now, at a church service called Holy Communion, each of the worshippers comes up to receive a piece of bread and a sip of wine.

GOOD FRIDAY, the day of Jesus' death, is a solemn day. We all go to church and the adults receive Holy Communion.

When we get home, we eat hot cross buns. They're made with sultanas and spices, and they have a cross on the top to remind us that Jesus died on a cross.

EASTER SUNDAY

TWO DAYS AFTER Good Friday is Easter Sunday, when we remember Jesus' resurrection. On the third day after Jesus was buried, his tomb was found to be empty. Christians believe that He rose from the dead (the Resurrection).

IT'S TRADITIONAL to have Easter eggs on this day as a celebration. They can be made of chocolate, or you can use real eggs and decorate them.

Here I'm making decorated eggs. First I have to blow the egg to make it hollow. I prick both ends with a pin, and carefully blow through one end to make the yolk and white come out of the other. Then, once the egg is hollow, I paint the shell.

EGGS ARE A SYMBOL of new life, so they help us remember the miracle of Jesus coming back to life. Forty days after Easter, He led His friends to the top of a hill. A low cloud covered the hilltop, and when it lifted, He was gone. We believe that He ascended to heaven.

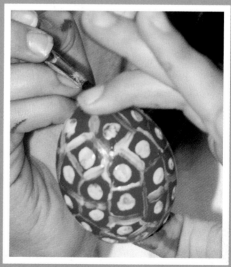

Food is extremely important in the Jewish religion. We have traditional dishes for each one of our festivals and strict rules about what we can and can't eat every day. Eating together with family and friends is one of the most important parts of our culture.

FOOD THAT JEWISH PEOPLE are allowed to eat is called *kosher* food. We buy our meat from a kosher butcher and we're not allowed to eat any meat that comes from a pig.

WE'RE ALSO NOT ALLOWED to eat meat and dairy products as part of the same meal. We have two sets of pans, plates and cutlery – one set for dairy meals and the other for meat meals. In my house, orange is for meat and blue is for dairy.

SHABBAT

OUR SABBATH, or *Shabbat*, is the most important part of the week. We rest and do no work for a whole day. We don't watch television or play music either, and our house feels very peaceful. Shabbat starts on Friday night as soon as it's dark. Mum lights two candles and says a prayer. Then a blessing is said over a cup of wine. Everyone has some wine – even the children.

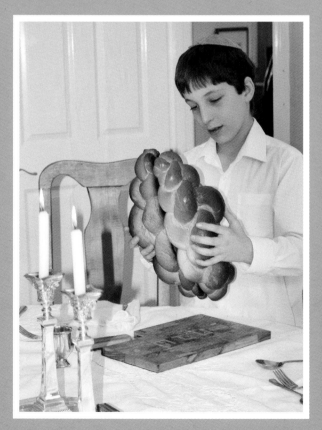

NEXT WE ALL go and wash our hands using a two-handled beaker kept especially for Shabbat. We say another blessing as we dry them.

Then the final blessing is said over two plaited loaves, called *challahs*. That's always my job. When I've said the blessing, I tear off a bit of challah for each person, dip it in salt and pass it round the table, piece by piece.

ROSH HASHANAH • YOM KIPPUR

The most holy time in the Jewish year is a 10-day period called the Days of Awe. During this time we try very hard to think about the bad things we've done in the past year and how we can do better in the future.

ROSH HASHANAH, our New Year, comes at the beginning of the 10 days. We eat apple dipped in honey, because we're hoping for a sweet year to come. It's traditional to eat a 'new fruit' as well – one that we haven't yet eaten that season.

THE DAYS OF AWE end with the most holy day of all: Yom Kippur, the Day of Repentance. It's a fast day, so adults aren't allowed to eat or drink anything at all. I won't have to fast till I'm 13, but for now I only eat simple food – no treats! Here, my sister and I are walking to synagogue. We spend nearly the whole of Yom Kippur there.

CHANUKAH

IN DECEMBER we celebrate Chanukah, the Festival of Lights. We remember the time 2,000 years ago when the Jewish people recaptured their holy temple from the Syrians. They only had enough oil to keep the eternal flame burning for one day, but by a miracle the oil lasted for eight days. So for eight days we light a special candlestick called a *Chanukiah*. We light one candle on the first day, two on the second, and so on, right up to eight candles.

DURING CHANUKAH we eat lots of different foods made with oil. Jam doughnuts are my favourite. To make them, I put a blob of jam in the middle of each circle of dough, then fold the dough around the jam. Afterwards, Mum fries them in hot oil.

DURING THE FESTIVAL of Purim, we celebrate the story of how Queen Esther saved the Jewish people from a wicked man called Haman who was plotting to kill them. Here, I am getting ready to go to a Purim fancy dress party. I'm making a basket of food to take with me. It's called *mishloach manot*. We give these baskets to our friends at Purim, and also to charity.

A FEW WEEKS AFTER PURIM comes Passover, or Pesach. We remember how the Jewish people escaped from slavery in Egypt thousands of years ago. We eat no bread during Passover and the night before it begins we search every corner of the house to clean it of crumbs. Here, Mum and I are doing traditional Passover cleaning – she lights the way with a candle and I sweep away the crumbs with a feather.

PASSOVER

ON THE FIRST TWO EVENINGS of Passover we have a meal called a *Seder*. On the table is a Seder plate, filled with special foods that symbolise different parts of the Passover story.

BEITZA
Roasted egg

KARPAS
Vegetable

CHAZERET
Bitter herbs

MAROR
More bitter herbs

SALT WATER

ZEROA
Shank bone

CHAROSET
Fruits, wine, honey, nuts and spices

WHEN THE JEWISH people fled from Egypt, they didn't have time to wait for their bread to rise before they left. That's why, during the eight days of Passover, we eat no bread — only *matzah*, which is a type of bread that hasn't risen. At the Seder meal, children are taught the story of how our people escaped.

ANEESA'S STORY

In Islam, food is central to our culture and it's really important to cook for our friends and relatives. But during one month of the year we're not allowed to eat at all from before dawn until sunset. We call this month Ramadan.

FOOD THAT MUSLIMS ARE ALLOWED TO EAT IS CALLED *HALAL*.
Here is the halal butcher where we buy our meat. We're not allowed to eat any meat that comes from a pig, as pigs are considered to be unclean. No one is allowed to drink alcohol, either, because we believe that we must take good care of our bodies.

RAMADAN

DURING THE MONTH of Ramadan, the grown-ups must not eat or drink from before dawn until sunset. I don't have to fast yet because I'm too young, but I just eat simple food during the day. At sunset, we 'open the fast' – that means everyone is [all]owed to eat something at last. [W]e always start with dates, and in my family we have fresh fruit as well.

MY MUM AND DAD, little brothers, sister, cousin and I all tuck in, and the food disappears very quickly. After that comes the sunset prayer, followed by the main meal. I try to stay up a bit later than usual during Ramadan, even if I have school the next day.

EID UL FITR

At the end of Ramadan we have a big celebration called Eid ul Fitr. We spend ages cooking delicious food so that we are prepared when our family and friends come round. My mum and dad buy me special new clothes, and I have my hands painted with *henna*, a plant dye.

IN THE EVENING, after we have opened our fast, we hurry outside to look for the new moon. We really hope to see it, because it means that Ramadan is over at last and Eid has begun. Then we phone the mosque and they confirm whether Eid has started, or whether we need to wait another day.

As soon as we know that it is Eid, we have a big rush to prepare everything for the friends and relatives who will visit tomorrow. There's lots of cooking to do.

HERE, I'M MAKING tandoori chicken. I put all the ingredients in a big bowl: tomato, garlic, chilli, lemon, mint sauce, herbs and spices, yoghurt and red colouring. Then I mix everything together and my hands turn bright red. It takes ages to wash them afterwards!

EID UL FITR

IN THE MORNING my dad and little brothers go to the mosque and my mum and I pray at home (though in many countries, women go to the mosque as well).

Then I prepare the *sivaiyyan* for breakfast. It's a mixture of vermicelli, butter, sugar, milk and cardamoms.

Next, my cousin paints beautiful patterns on my hands with henna.

all

AS SOON AS the others get back from the mosque, everyone greets each other, saying *Eid Mubarik!* which means 'Happy Festival!', and men and boys give each other three hugs.

My brothers sweeten their mouths with the sivaiyyan. They say a special prayer to thank Allah for the food.

EID UL FITR

THE MEAL IS ready for our visitors. You can see my tandoori chicken in the middle. Here's what all the different dishes are:

CHICKEN TIKKA

SALAD

CHICKEN CURRY

TANDOORI CHICKEN

RAITA
Yogurt with cucumber, onion and tomato

KHEER
Milk, sugar and rice

RICE WITH VEGETABLES

EID UL FITR • EID UL ADHA

IT'S TIME FOR EVERYONE to eat. After we've finished, we go to my auntie's, then my cousin's. It's important to accept the food we're offered, so I have to eat something in each home, even if I'm completely full up!

EID UL FITR is also known as Little Eid. This is followed just over two months later by Eid ul Adha, or Big Eid, when every Muslim family sacrifices an animal and shares the meat — one-third for themselves, one-third for relatives and one-third for the poor. We remember the time when Allah appeared to the Prophet Ibrahim and told him to sacrifice his son. As the Prophet Ibrahim was about to do so, Allah stopped him. We sacrifice an animal to remember that the Prophet Ibrahim was willing to give to Allah what was most precious to him.

At both Eids we celebrate, pray, cook, welcome guests to eat in our home, and visit family and friends. It's a time to thank Allah for all He has blessed us with and to share what He has given us with others.

FRANCIS' STORY

In my faith, we follow the teachings of the Buddha, a spiritual leader from Ancient India. He taught us how to lead our lives in the best possible way.

I AM AT a family weekend at Amaravati Buddhist Monastery. We help cook communal meals together, we learn about Buddhism together, we meditate together.

JUST AS IN the time of the Buddha, the monks and nuns are not allowed to buy, grow or cook their own food. They depend on the lay community (non-monks/nuns) to provide it for them. These shopping bags contain food and other supplies that have been donated.

PREPARING LUNCH

I'M HELPING TO MAKE lunch in the monastery kitchen. I like taking part in the food preparations – it's a way to carry out a good act, to do something for somebody else. It isn't so important what kind of food we prepare. What counts is that we are cooking together with a giving heart, knowing that this food will be offered to the monks and nuns and shared among us.

WHEN IT'S TIME TO EAT, I ring the bell to let everybody know that the meal is being offered. It's really important to make sure the monks and nuns know that the meal is ready. They may only eat what is formally offered to them, and this is their final meal of the day, so if they miss it, they won't get another chance to eat until tomorrow!

DANA

BEFORE WE BEGIN, we join hands to reflect on the meal we are about to eat and to express our gratitude for how it has reached us.

THEN, AS THE MONKS AND NUNS file past, we each put a little food into their bowls. The offering, the generosity, is called *dana*, and to give food is considered an honour.

The food that is offered is all mixed up together in the same bowl. The monks and nuns consider food, although enjoyable, as something to nourish them, to help their bodies live. They have to finish their meal by midday.

VESAK

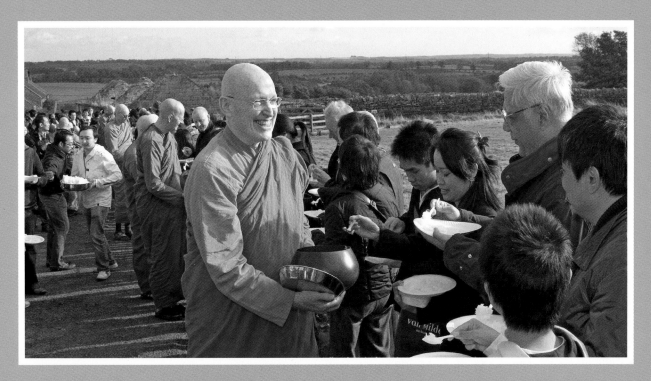

A FEW WEEKS after the family weekend, I go back to the monastery for the festival of Vesak. It's a time for celebrating the birth, death and enlightenment of the Buddha. This is one of my favourite times of year, when the lay community participates in a dana ceremony. Everyone stands in a line, and as the monks and nuns pass by, we spoon a little rice into each bowl.

AT VESAK, just as on every visit to the monastery, we remind ourselves of the five precepts – the five guidelines for living together:

- Don't harm or kill living beings.
- Don't take things that don't belong to you.
- Don't indulge in sexual misconduct.
- Don't speak unkindly or tell lies.
- Don't take drugs or alcohol.

We remember the Buddha's message that we can learn to live a life of generosity, virtue and wisdom.

AKHIL'S STORY

Hindus believe it's important to remember that our food comes from Mother Earth. We don't eat beef because we also see the cow as our mother. Many of us are vegetarian because we believe that we shouldn't injure any living creature. We call this *ahimsa* (non-violence).

EVERY WEEK I go with my family to the temple – the *mandir*. The first thing I do is ring the temple bell. This is a way of announcing to God that I've come to offer my prayers.

AT THE TEMPLE ALTAR, the priest offers food to the *murtis*. A murti is an image representing God. Then comes the *arti* ceremony, which you can see here, also called the Ceremony of Lights. The priest rings a bell and offers incense, a flower, water and a lamp to the murti, moving them in circles clockwise.

WORSHIP

AFTER THE ARTI, the priest and temple volunteers share the food that has been offered with the worshippers. This food is called *prasad*, which means 'God's grace' or sanctified food. Here I am being given a morsel of prasad from a *thali* – a plate with small dishes containing several types of food.

AS WELL AS going to the temple, we have a shrine in our home where we offer food to a murti of Shrinathji every day. There are many Hindu gods and goddesses, and most families have their favourite. Ours is Shrinathji, which is another name for Krishna. We worship the murti as our Supreme Being or Lord Almighty.

DIWALI

FOR MOST HINDUS, the most important festival is Diwali, the Festival of Lights. It celebrates the return home of Prince Rama, and of his wife Sita, who had been kidnapped by Ravana, the demon king. It's all about good winning over evil, and light driving away darkness.

AT DIWALI we hold firework displays and put out lamps called *divas* to light the way home for Rama and Sita. The lamps contain *ghee* (butter oil) which is also important in Hindu cooking.

We decorate our houses, give presents and cards, and wear new clothes.

PEOPLE MAKE beautiful *rangoli* patterns in the temple or outside their homes. These can either be made with coloured rice and other grains, or drawn with coloured chalk. We hope that the goddess Lakshmi will see the beautiful patterns and come to visit us.

DIWALI

MY MUM AND GRANDMA have been cooking all day to make our Diwali meal. These are the things we're going to eat.

SEV
Salty fried snack

AAMRAS
Mango pulp

LADDOO
Sweets

ALMONDS

KHURME
Savoury snack

PEDA, MAKHAN, BADA AND COCONUT BARFI
Sweets

FRESH FRUITS

MATHRI
Flaky crackers

I SIT DOWN with my mum and dad, grandma and my little brother to enjoy the meal. We use all our best silverware and we each have a thali containing lots of little dishes.

HOLI

THE FESTIVAL OF HOLI celebrates the coming of spring. The day before Holi is called Holika Dahan. We light bonfires on that day in memory of a boy called Prahlada. He was carried into a terrible fire by a demoness called Holika, but he escaped without any injuries, while evil Holika burned to death.

I'M HELPING to prepare the evening meal. I'm grinding cardamom to make *kheer*, a sweet dish usually made wtih milk, sugar and rice. On Holika Dahan, we're not allowed to eat any grains or pulses – and that includes rice. So I'm using sago instead – it's a type of starch.

THE MEAL is ready. There's kheer, potatoes and a dish called *khichdi*, made from sago, potatoes and peanuts. There are also nuts and fruit.

HOLI

THE NEXT DAY IS HOLI. We eat lots of sweets and light a big bonfire. At the temple we all squirt coloured powder at each other – even the adults! We do it to remember that the god Krishna liked to play pranks. There's a huge mess, but we wear old clothes and nobody cares!

Afterwards, we have a shower to wash the colour away. Then we sit down for a feast which ends with a special dessert called *shrikhand*, made from yogurt.

ॐ • • • • • HINDU • • • • •

TAVLEEN'S STORY

In the Sikh religion, food is part of every religious ceremony. At the end of each service we share a meal called the *langar*. We believe that we're all part of God's family, so we sit and eat together, just like any other family.

IT'S A FESTIVAL DAY today – the birthday of the 10th Guru, Gobind Singh, who lived about 400 years ago. The Gurus were people who showed us how we should live our lives.

MY FAMILY IS TAKING a turn to buy the food for the langar and help prepare it, so Mum and I go shopping early in the morning. I choose some coriander to go in the vegetable curry while Mum gets the rest of the ingredients. Then she lets me buy some *jalebi*, my favourite sweets.

Afterwards, we rush home to change into our best clothes for the festival.

PREPARING THE LANGAR

WHEN WE REACH the *gurdwara* (the temple), breakfast is ready waiting for us. As soon as we've finished eating, it's time to start preparing the langar.

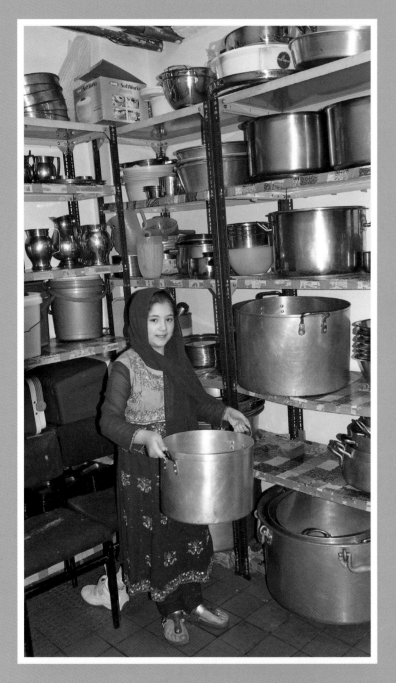

THERE ARE GOING to be a lot of people in the gurdwara today, because it's a festival. I'm sent to choose a big pot to make the chickpea curry. It's important that everyone who visits the gurdwara has plenty to eat, so the kitchen has enormous pans for cooking huge amounts of food.

The food in the gurdwara is always vegetarian so that anyone can eat it, whatever their faith. It's important to us that everyone feels welcome.

SIKH

KRAH PRASHAD • LANGAR

MY BROTHER DEVAN and I are busy preparing the *krah prashad*. This is made from flour, sugar and water, and it's given to everyone at the end of the prayers. It tastes sweet, to signify the sweetness of God's grace.

You can see that Devan is wearing a cloth over his hair. It's called a *patka*. Sikhs aren't allowed to cut their hair, so Devan's patka keeps his long hair clean and tidy.

NEXT WE STIR the *gulab jamun*. These are dough balls in a sugary syrup, and they're going to be our dessert.

KRAH PRASHAD • LANGAR

AT LAST the cooking is done and we go to the prayer service. At the end of the service, one of the men stirs the krah prashad with his *kirpan* (sword), then everyone cups their hands to receive it.

AND THEN THE BEST BIT – the langar! Everyone is given a tray of food (including the gulab jamun that Devan and I helped to make) and we take it to the gurdwara dining-room.

A lot of hard work goes into making and giving food to all the people who come to the gurdwara. We Sikhs think that every type of work is valuable, so men, women and children share the cooking and cleaning equally.

LANGAR

ALOO AND VATAIUN CURRY
Potato and aubergine

RICE PUDDING

APPLE

GULAB JAMUN
Sweet dough balls

CHHOLE CURRY
With chick peas

PURI
Bread

SALAD

WHEN WE'RE eating the langar, everyone sits in long rows. This shows that we're all equal – no one is more important than anyone else.

VAISAKHI

ABOUT THREE MONTHS after the birthday of Guru Gobind Singh, the festival of Vaisakhi takes place. It's one of the most important festivals in the Sikh year. It marks the New Year, and also the time when Guru Gobind Singh set up the *khalsa*, our Sikh community. Children are given lots of sweets, and the gurdwaras are full of people who come to pray and celebrate.

HERE WE ARE at one of the Vaisakhi street celebrations. There are hundreds of people here from all religions. There's music and *bhangra* dancing, martial arts, and, most importantly, the langar, which is free for everyone who wants to join us and eat.

SIKH

RECIPES

Christian

PANCAKES

- 110g/4oz plain flour • pinch of salt
- 3 eggs • 225ml/8fl oz milk
- 50g/2oz butter plus a little extra for greasing the frying pan

- Take a large mixing bowl and sift in the flour and salt.
- Break in the eggs and whisk them into the mixture.
- Gradually whisk in the milk to make a smooth batter.
- With the help of a grown-up, melt the butter in a pan, then whisk it into the batter, leaving a little for greasing the pancake pan.
- Brush the base of a frying pan with some melted butter. There should be just enough to thinly coat the pan.
- Heat the pan, then spoon in some batter with a ladle.
- Tip the pan from side to side so that the base is evenly coated.
- Cook for about half a minute until the pancake is light brown underneath and lifts up easily from the pan. Then flip it over using a palette knife or fish slice.
- Cook the other side until brown, then slide the pancake out of the pan on to a plate.

You can eat pancakes with lots of different fillings — sweet or savoury. Try them with lemon and sugar, chocolate spread or grated cheese. Put on the filling, then roll them up or fold them into quarters.

Jewish

HONEY CAKE

- 175g/6oz plain flour
- 75g/3oz caster sugar
- 1 level tsp bicarbonate of soda
- 1 tsp mixed spice
- ½ tsp ground ginger
- ½ tsp ground cinnamon
- 225g/8oz clear honey
- 4 tbsp sunflower oil
- 2 eggs
- grated rind of an orange
- 125ml/4fl oz orange juice
- 50g/2oz chopped walnuts

- Mix together the flour, sugar, mixed spice, ginger and cinnamon.
- Add the honey, oil, rind, eggs and the bicarbonate of soda dissolved in the orange juice.
- Beat well together until smooth.
- Stir in the nuts and pour the mixture into a 25x20x5cm/10x8x2in tin lined with silicone paper.
- Ask a grown-up to bake it at 180°C/350°F/ gas mark 4 for 45-55 minutes, or until firm to touch. A skewer inserted in the middle should come out clean.
- Remove from the oven and leave to cool.
- When completely cold, wrap tightly in foil.

Honey cake improves with keeping, so if possible, store at room temperature and wait 4-5 days before eating.

RECITES

Muslim

PAKORAS

- 2 large onions • 2 tbsp finely chopped fresh coriander • salt to taste • ½ tsp baking powder • 4 tbsp gram flour • sunflower or vegetable oil for frying

- Put the gram flour in a bowl.
- Mix with about 8 tbsp water to make a paste.
- Make sure all the knobbly bits of gram flour are 'squashed' so the paste is smooth.
- Finely slice the onions.
- Add the chopped coriander and mix the onions and coriander with the paste.
- Add the baking powder.
- Add salt to taste.
- Ask a grown-up to drop tablespoons of the batter into hot oil and deep fry until crisp and golden, turning the pakoras over to fry both sides.
- Remove from the pan with a slotted spoon and drain on a kitchen towel.

Hindu

COCONUT BARFI

- 100g/3.5oz desiccated coconut
- 100g/3.5oz milk powder
- 100g/3.5oz caster sugar
- ¼ tsp cardamom powder or ground cardamom seeds

- Mix the coconut and the milk powder, and put aside.
- Prepare the syrup by adding 4 fl oz water to the sugar in a pan.
- Ask a grown-up to heat the mixture until the sugar melts.
- Add the coconut and milk powder to the syrup, along with the cardamom powder.
- Spread the mixture on to a plate and cover it.
- Allow to cool so it can be handled.
- Cut into small squares.

Sikh

PURIS

- 250g/9oz wholemeal flour
- vegetable oil for frying
- salt to taste

- Put the flour and salt in a large bowl, and slowly add enough water to make a firm dough.
- Knead the dough until smooth.
- Cover the bowl and let the dough rest for 1 hour.
- Knead the dough a little more, then divide it into small balls.
- Brush the balls with a little vegetable oil and roll into circles of about 13cm/5in across.
- Ask a grown-up to deep-fry the puris, one at a time, in hot vegetable oil.
- After a few seconds, the puri will puff up.
- Flip it over and cook it on the other side until golden brown.
- Serve straight away.

GLOSSARY

Ahimsa
Hindu concept of non-violence and respect for life

Arti
Hindu ceremony. Incense, a lamp and flowers are offered to the murti

Bhangra
Punjabi folk dance

Challah
Plaited loaf eaten on the Jewish Sabbath

Chanukiah
Nine-pronged candlestick used at the Jewish festival of Chanukah

Christingle
Orange studded with symbolic objects, used by Christians for the Christingle ceremony

Dana
Buddhist term for the act of giving

Diva
Lamp used at Diwali

Ghee
Clarified butter, used by Hindus in lamps and cooking

Gurdwara
Sikh temple

Halal
'Permitted'. Usually refers to meat prepared according to Muslim guidelines

Holy Communion
The Christian act of worship, also called the Eucharist, where bread is eaten and wine drunk to represent Jesus Christ's body and blood

Hot cross bun
Bun containing dried fruits and marked with a cross on the top, traditionally eaten on Good Friday

Khalsa
Community of Sikhs who have undergone the sacred Amrit Ceremony initiated by Guru Gobind Singh

Kheer
Sweet dish made with milk, sugar and rice

Kirpan
A sword worn as a symbol to defend the weak

Kosher
Term for food permitted for Jewish people

Krah prashad
A food made from flour, sugar and water received at the end of prayers in the Sikh gurdwara

Langar
Meal eaten in the Sikh gurdwara

Mandir
Hindu temple

Matzah
Flat, unleavened bread eaten by Jewish people at Passover

Mishloach Manot
Basket of food given to friends or to charity at the festival of Purim

Murti
Sacred Hindu statue representing God

Patka
Turban worn by young Sikh boys to keep their long hair clean and tidy

Puja
Hindu worship

Rangoli
Pattern made for Diwali out of coloured grains or chalk

Seder
Ceremonial meal eaten on the first two evenings of Passover, when Jewish people tell the story of the flight of the Israelites from slavery in Egypt

Sivaiyyan
Dish traditionally eaten for breakfast at Eid, containing vermicelli, butter, sugar, milk and cardamoms

Thali
Large metal plate holding several small eating bowls

INDEX